Herb the Spinning Hamster

Broadfield C P School
Rochdale

Meet Herb the Spinning Hamster.

He zooms and spins near planets and stars.

Herb helps if bad things happen.

Never fear if I am near!

Rocket Dog frightens Comet Cat.
I will get you!
Zoom!
Never fear! I am near!

Fox frightens all of the moon rabbits.

Clear off, Fox!

Thank you, Herb!

Herb sees a big monster.
It is sure to attack!

I am going in!

Grrr!

Herb is quick.
He nips the monster.

Ow! That hurts!

That was a shock! I am going!

Off you go, monster!